THE SECRET POWER OF

FORGIVENESS

Wendy Bustin

Copyright © 2020 by Wendy Bustin

THE SECRET POWER OF FORGIVENESS

Printed in the United States of America

ISBN 978-1-7350275-2-4

All rights are reserved solely by the author. The author declares that the contents are original and do not infringe on the rights of any other person.

No part of this book may be reproduced in any form except with permission from the author. The views in this book are not necessarily the views of the publisher.

DEDICATION

To my parents, Gerald and Roane Bustin, who have taught me by example that choosing forgiveness and love instead of revenge and hate is always the right choice. Thanks for the many years of prayers when it looked like I would never truly come to know God. Thanks for passing on to me such a godly heritage and legacy by sharing the love of God with not only me but Nations around the world.

To my brother Gary, who I so admire because although you had many opportunities to become bitter you choose to become better and have always encouraged me to take the high road. I am so proud of you and all you have done in Papua New Guinea through Tribal Foundation to make such a huge difference in the lives of those often overlooked by society. You are a living example of the difference one life with a purpose can make!

THE SECRET POWER OF FORGIVENESS

To my son Nick, you are one of my greatest gifts from God. Having you as my son helped me to understand God's love more. It also gave me the courage to conquer demons in my own life so that I could teach you by example that it is possible through God to live a victorious life. You have overcome more in your young life than many have, but I know God has great plans for you and I love your heart for helping others. I am so grateful God has allowed me to be your mother and am beyond thankful for the privilege of loving you.

I also dedicate this book to so many people who have inspired me and encouraged me along my journey. People who have paid a huge price to become all God called them to be and as a result motivated me to also commit to paying that price. One of those people is Real Talk Kim. Much like me she has gone through a lot of challenges but has overcome them with God's help and is a mighty warrior in the Kingdom of God. I am so grateful not only for her example but for her willingness to write the forward of this book.

Lastly, I dedicate this book to my best friend and lover of my soul, who never gave up on me even when I gave up and walked away in rejection and despair. You have loved me even when I felt unlovable, never left me even when I felt forsaken, and showed me over time who You really are and who I am in You. You paid a price for me that is incomprehensible and taught me how valued and loved I am by you and by my Heavenly Father. I thank you, Jesus for walking this journey ahead of me and beside me, and for teaching me the secret power of forgiveness through your Holy Spirit.

TABLE OF CONTENTS

INTRODUCTION... vii
FOREWORD... xi
CHAPTER 1- KNOCKED OFF MY HIGH HORSE....13
CHAPTER 2- RUNNING FROM GOD.................. 29
CHAPTER 3- DARKEST DAYS OF MY LIFE.........34
CHAPTER 4- DISCOVERING WHAT
              FORGIVENESS IS..........................65
CHAPTER 5- FORGIVE FOR THE HEALTH
              OF IT.. 75
CHAPTER 6- LETTING YOURSELF OFF
              THE HOOK................................ 81
CHAPTER 7- THE SECRET POWER OF
              FORGIVENESS........................... 89
CHAPTER 8- GAINING THE RIGHT PERSPECTIVE
              OF THE LORD........................... 94
CHAPTER 9- TOTAL WELLNESS..................... 101
CHAPTER 10- THE POWER OF FORGIVENESS... 111
CHAPTER 11- CHOOSING FORGIVENESS......... 118

INTRODUCTION

I heard this story from a friend of mine about a professor who taught college kids about business and how to make money. The professor asked this friend of mine, who has made millions buying fixer-upper homes to come teach the class for a week.

My friend agreed to come but charged each student that wanted to attend the class $1,500 for the week. When my friend got there, he found out that the professor, who taught business, had never even owned a business. He had been telling the students he did not really believe people could make money flipping houses. The professor had the knowledge of it, but no real experience actually doing it. My friend told the class that if they did three specific things, he would not only teach them how to do it, but he would help them do it. The three things were seemingly easy to follow but like so many things, they require focus, consistence and diligence.

My friend told them to show up and be ready to start each class on time, pay attention, and ask lots of questions. He gave them his word that if they would do that, he would personally help them get started learning what they needed to know to be successful. He then told me later that he was shocked to see how many people paid the money to take the class, and didn't pay attention or wasted their time.

At the end of the week, those who were serious and followed his guidance gained access to the secrets that made him successful.

My friend also told them one more thing. He said that he had shown up a week before the class started, found a house in that area that needed to be fixed up, and he bought it. During that week and the next week that he was teaching them, he had hired a crew to fix it up and he sold it, making a profit of $40,000.

He then went on to say to be careful who you listen to; because while your professor believed selling a house in that area was impossible, I made it work and was able to reap the benefits. Then he told all the students who had done the three things he had asked at the beginning of the week to please stand, and he gave them back their $1,500 to help them start buying their first property.

He told the other ones who had failed to show up on time and who had not paid attention or asked questions that he was keeping their money and donating it to a charity because he didn't need it. He had made his own that week and wanted them to learn a lesson.

That is the difference between really knowing something and just having the knowledge of it. There are lots of people walking around with 'book smarts' but they don't really know how to apply it because they either lack common sense or life experience. It is so much easier to tell someone what they should do rather than actually doing it yourself.

The secrets I want to share with you in this book are things I personally have learned through years of hard knocks. I have chosen to be transparent in this book because until you know someone's story, you can't truly relate to them and know that what they are saying is true. You really must be careful who you allow to speak into your life.

THE SECRET POWER OF FORGIVENESS

If you read this book with an open heart and really pay attention, it can save you years of heartache, pain, and needless struggle. Or you may be like the other kids in that class and learn the lesson the hard way but, it will cost you dearly. I should know because that is how I came to learn the secret power of forgiveness.

FOREWORD

This awesome book is a Freedom Giver. When Wendy asked me to do her forward for this incredible book on FORGIVENESS, I jumped at it for two reasons. The first reason is I believe blessings and life are connected to our heart posture and forgiveness. Secondly, I literally watch this great woman of God walk in it daily. Wendy is the poster child for loving everyone no matter what the circumstances. This is a jewel of wisdom you must add to your treasure box.

Forgiveness is so crucial because the Bible tells us we must walk in it to receive the blessings that God has stored up for us even though many times it's a difficult task. When someone you love or believed would never hurt you, hurts you, it's so devastating and can delay your destiny for the simple fact that it caused a wound that is so deep it's hard to see your way out beyond the pain.

This incredible book on FORGIVENESS will bring forth a

trajectory shift for you. It will change your perspective on the matter. Both Wendy and I are examples of overcoming and forgiving. It matters. Both of us were raised in preacher's homes, lived in glass houses and discovered the importance of choosing to forgive, regardless of how we felt.

This book will open your eyes to realize that the pain you feel may not be your fault, but the healing is your responsibility. If you don't take the steps to forgive, you will live the rest of your life bleeding on people who didn't cut you. So just forgive. Forgiveness is not for the perpetrator, but it is for YOU. Also, I have discovered that you can forgive someone and not want anything to do with them. People need to understand that forgiveness is for past reconciliation and not for future consideration.

As you read this book, please keep an open mind to receive the words that Wendy has written for you. It is going to set your soul on fire.

Real Talk Kim

Chapter 1: Knocked Off My High Horse

Most of my life, I have learned things the hard way. Call it being stubborn or hard-headed, but I always seemed to jump in feet first and learn by doing rather than by just being told. The good news is that I did learn those lessons, so the time was not lost, even though it might have been a lot easier than it would have been had I just listened.

There is a scripture in the Bible that says, "My people perish for lack of knowledge." It is talking about God's people. Good people who love God perish because they don't have the knowledge, they need to navigate the life lessons they must learn. So, how do we get that knowledge? We get it by learning it ahead of time from others or by experiencing it.

One of those lessons for me was about judging others. I didn't even know at the time that was what I was doing. I just looked at others going through things and thought "I would never do that." Divorce was one of those areas for me.

You see, I was born into a family from a long line of missionaries and preachers on both sides. In fact, my parents were missionaries in Papua New Guinea when I was born and so my whole life growing up I had been involved in church and ministry. Hardly anyone in my family, going back several generations, had ever been divorced and that was something I was sure I would never do. When it was time for me to get married, my own parents had been together 21 years and I had never seen them fight.

So, prior to me getting married, I used to look at others going through tough marriages or getting a divorce and would say, "Wow, that will never happen to me! I will never get a divorce because when I get married, I will just treat my husband so good that he will always be happy." It never occurred to me that my husband might not do the same thing and that he might play a huge part in getting a divorce. From my high and mighty perch, I would look down my nose at others and pity them but think "I will never be like them." Little did I know that God was going to allow me to get knocked off that perch nor did I anticipate how thankful or grateful I would be to God for teaching me this lesson.

Up until my late teens, I didn't recall really needing to know the secret power of forgiveness. Sure, I had people in my life growing up that I had to forgive but it was mainly from misunderstandings, bullying, and things that didn't require real power to forgive.

I had also been hurt by so called "church people" who placed high expectations on me but then seem to try to point out my faults/things I did wrong at the same time. It felt like they wanted me to fail so they could justify their own life by saying "See, even a preacher/missionary's kid can't live up to all the expectations."

From as far back as I can remember, our family was either in another country helping the people starting schools, clinics, and churches, and teaching them to survive, or we were traveling here in the States as my Father would speak at different churches across the country. When we were in the USA, we were nearly always on the road. Sometimes we stayed in a travel trailer but most of the time we stayed with people who had been kind enough to keep us for the week or two my Father was preaching. That made for an interesting life with many crazy dynamics. I learned from an early age about the diversity of people. I learned to be comfortable in a grass hut in the jungles of Papua New Guinea or in the home of an Ambassador.

I had many adventures as a kid and would not trade my life or the lessons I learned along the way for anything. However, it also brought with it a lot of unique challenges. Because of who my father was, people's expectations of me and my brother were higher than that of so called "normal kids" and oftentimes those expectations were too high for any kid to live up to.

By the time I was in college I was totally worn out from the "fish bowl" I felt I had lived in for way too long, and was desperate to get out and have the chance to live life without feeling the constant judgment and watching eyes of everyone I knew. I felt helpless to live up to people's expectations any longer, so when a man seven years my senior came along and began to intentionally sweep me off my feet, I saw it as a possible way of escape.

Over the course of the year that we dated I saw plenty of red flags, but each time made some sort of excuse for him and his behavior. I rationalized that it would be easier to deal with one person's expectations rather than so many others. As we drew closer to the wedding date, I seriously began to reconsider and even talked to a couple of people about canceling the wedding. My fiancé's mother sensed my hesitation and began doing her best to convince me that this was a "God thing" and that she had visions that we were meant to be together. His brother convinced me that if I ended the relationship, that my then fiancé would end his life.

Being a naive 20-year-old who truly did not want to disappoint anyone, much less cause someone to end their life, I chose to go through with it despite my many concerns. Besides, I was going to be the best wife I could be and how could anyone not love a wife like that, right? Years later I found out there were people who really knew him who were taking bets on whether I would find out the truth about him before I married him, but they didn't feel the need to tell me ahead of time.

Almost from the start of the honeymoon, as we drove away, he was verbally abusive and that started a journey of over four years where I lived in an emotional, sometimes physical, and definitely spiritual hell on earth. From a spiritual standpoint, it wasn't that God ever abandoned me; it was that my spirit became so crushed that I almost lost myself and, in the process, any connection to God.

What I had thought was going to be my escape from the prying eyes of people was what my ex-husband thought was going to be his instant claim to fame. Almost from the start, he began to tell me that the only reason he married me was for the notoriety he was going to get from being married to the daughter of my father. On multiple occasions, he bragged to others that he had married into a well-known family.

THE SECRET POWER OF FORGIVENESS

Many other times he told me I was lucky he married me because no one else would have wanted to, and the only reason he did was because he wanted a huge ministry like my father's. He believed he could have that if he was connected to my father in some way. I just happened to be a means to an end with him.

Right from the start, he began to physically abuse me and was constantly in my face screaming at me for what a failure I was in general but especially as a wife. Although I was still in college, working full-time and taking care of all my duties as a wife, nothing was good enough or made him happy in any way.

One afternoon he became even more angry than usual and literally picked me up. I was 110 lbs. at the time and he threw me out the front door onto the ground outside and told me to leave and never come back.

I was heartbroken. How was I to explain to all those watching eyes and my parents that, despite my best efforts, I could not succeed as a wife and my husband wanted me to leave? I drove around and sat in my car, broken and shattered, for hours wondering what to do. It finally dawned on me that maybe I could call one of the pastors at the church we attended who had performed our wedding.

When I reached out to him, he said "Yes, please come in at 6:00 p.m." but little did I know, he had already received a call from my now ex-husband and they had already talked. So, when I got there before I could explain anything the pastor said to me, "You need to go home and work on being a better wife and understand that sometimes men get upset and you should not provoke them. If you would just work on being more submissive, then you would have a better marriage."

I left that meeting with my spirit crushed even more and my body aching from feeling totally alone in the world.

My now ex-husband left that meeting with more ammunition to use against me, because now he knew his actions would have no consequences and that he could just demand that I become more submissive.

I knew I could have told my father and he would have defended me. There were occasions where a family member saw the bruises and asked me what had happened.

THE SECRET POWER OF FORGIVENESS

I am sure they didn't recognize that they were coming from him because when they asked me, it was in front of him. I gave them some excuse about falling over boxes and then they dropped it. I didn't elaborate that it was because I had been pushed. When we got home the physical abuse/violence continued. I learned then to never ask someone you suspect might be in an abusive relationship about it in front of or around the abuser.

I quickly learned that the judgmental high horse I had sat on for so long regarding anyone in marriage problems was beginning to crumble and sometimes you can do everything in your power to make a marriage work and it is still not going to survive . I have come to believe that if both people are committed and willing, they can come back from nearly anything and it is so much better to fight for a marriage then to go through the heartbreak of divorce if at all possible. However, living in abuse is never the answer and sometimes divorce is your only choice.

Not long after that, I finally demanded the physical abuse to stop or I was going to tell everyone I knew. Since he wanted prestige, and fame he stopped the physical abuse. However, then I soon realized that saying we said as kids was so wrong "Sticks and stones will break my bones but words can never harm me." Words do harm us and can crush the very life out of our spirit much more than even physical abuse. You see when there is physical abuse you can see the bruises and sometimes others see them as well so you know the event actually happen.

However when there is verbal abuse you begin to think you are losing your mind, especially when the abuser begins to tell you, after the fact, that you imagined or misinterpreted what was said. In this case, my ex was a master manipulator and would scream and yell at me in private, telling me things like "everyone would be better off if you were dead." Then in front of others, he would give me flowers or a dress or tell them how lucky he was to be married to me. They all believed him and when I seemed less than enthused, they would ask me what was wrong with me. They said that I had such a loving husband yet didn't appear to appreciate him. He then would play the sympathy card and convince them that I had emotional issues and he was trying to love me through them. Meanwhile, at home, he would scream at me and tell me how much he wished I would just put everyone out of their misery and end my life.

If I could go back now and give myself advice, I would say to get help, talk to your Dad, and truly tell him what is going on. However, at the time, I was like many people in abusive relationships and felt the indescribable need to protect the very person abusing me. I also didn't want to admit to being a failure by telling others since I felt that somehow, I had failed to make him love me and therefore had failed at the marriage.

For several years I lived with that abuse and begin to question my own sanity because when I would tell him it had to stop, he would tell me he didn't know what I was talking about and acted as if it was all in my mind. In my confused state of being so emotionally beat down, with my spirit literally dying inside and feeling like no one else noticed what was going on but me, I began to believe his words that everyone would be better off if I was gone. He even quoted scripture taken out of context to try and persuade me to go ahead and end my life. He told me that it would be better for me to end it all than for me to ruin his chance at a ministry or my father's ministry. He failed to explain how my being alive was hindering either of their ministries. However, when you have gone through abuse for so long, you begin to believe the lies of your abuser and mistake them for truth.

We were living at the headquarters of my father's ministry in Summerfield, Florida at the time. I began to feel that nothing I could do was right, feeling like a failure as a wife and a worthless individual, and that I was only hindering the ministry and the lives around me.

One night, as my ex began to scream and yell at me again, he handed me a bottle of pills saying "just put us all out of our misery and end it all," so I decided to take him up on it. It wasn't that I wanted to end my life but he had me really made me believe that I would be doing the world a favor if I just removed myself from their lives.

I took the bottle and planned on ending it, but decided to make one last phone call to a friend. As I sobbed into the phone and told her goodbye she had the presence of mind to get another friend on the phone and the two of them convinced me not to do it. I then called another

THE SECRET POWER OF FORGIVENESS

friend who got me a train ticket and a counselor who was willing to see me for free. I honestly believe those three friends saved my life that night.

On the way to the train my ex, who was mad that I was going, continued to yell at me and try to convince me of all sorts of calamities that would happen to me if I got on the train. He threatened, cajoled, and did his best to scare me into not going but I went on anyway.

I got on the train scared, broken, and feeling totally lost to the world. I was preparing for a long, lonely ride and then a young lady got on with a seat next to mine. She clearly looked the part of what I had been raised to believe a "Christian" looked like. However, she evidently didn't think I did and as she sat down beside me, she did her best to gather her skirts about her and scoot as far away from me as possible as though I would have contaminated her.

As I sat there in my seat, I couldn't help but think that if she really knew God, she could have shown kindness to me during one of the worst times in my life. Instead, she showed contempt because I didn't look like her. I asked

God to never allow me to forget that time because I never wanted to represent Him in such an awful way.

After fifty hours of travelling with many layovers and delays, I made it to Indiana. It was during that time I clearly heard God ask me if I was willing to obey Him regardless of what others would think. He clearly showed me I needed to get out of that marriage. I argued with God and told Him all the reasons why that could not possibly be Him. I finally surrendered to the idea that I would go back home and try to seek counseling with my then husband and if he refused to get help, I would leave. I soon learned that delayed obedience is still disobedience, and not listening to God when I should have resulted in a lot more heartache and decisions that I think God was trying to spare me from had I listened right away.

I did go back and we attempted counseling but each time my ex would end up mad at the counselor and want a new counselor until we had gone through five Christian counselors. Every one of them told me that if I didn't leave, I would end up dead.

THE SECRET POWER OF FORGIVENESS

Finally, through a series of events, I did end up leaving and when I did, I felt even more heartache and pain than before. Not only was I having to start over and try and figure out how to do things all on my own, but the very people who were supposed to show me God's love " Church People" failed me.

People I had once considered aunts and uncles those who I had grown up with in church never once asked me what they could do to help while I was going through pain. I received one letter from a dear elder lady telling me I was going straight to hell. While still more totally disassociated and ostracized me as if I had committed some heinous crime. So, not only was I going through the divorce with my ex but I felt like I was literally losing everyone that I had counted on for emotional support and love. Not one of them asked me what happened or why I was leaving. They just assumed the worse and wrote me off.

What was worse was that the very thing I had feared the most -harming my Father's ministry-seemed to happen. He and my mother were stuck between a rock and a hard place. Even though I was their daughter, their friends and other church people expected them to distance themselves from me and seem to judge them for my leaving.

I went through several years of feeling like I had hurt everyone I loved and let everyone down. I felt totally alone and abandoned by both God and man. During that time, I told God that if I had to be like those "Christians" and treat others like that! Then I wanted nothing to do with Him or them. I found that people who had not grown up in church were, a lot of the time, kinder and more compassionate than those who claimed to be Christians.

I spent years running from God and being totally disconnected from nearly everyone I knew, other than family, because I had no desire to live with the constant judgment and rejection, they showed me. It wasn't until years later that some of those same people told me they didn't know how I had lived under that abuse. They had witnessed and even heard him shouting at me on a regular basis and told me "we would not have survived it." Yet, they never once stepped in or even let me know they were aware that I was hurting.

Chapter 2: Running from God

During those years I was running from God, I met and married my second husband. I figured since I had married a "church boy" the first time around and that didn't work out I shouldn't make that a criteria the second time. That was another big mistake, and I spent years married to a man I loved but who thought it was okay to cheat on me and do drugs. He would get angry when I wanted to go to church and did everything to talk me into not going.

Although we had many happy times eventually life with him became filled with turmoil and extreme heartache. I had not planned on having a child with him because there seemed to be too many issues but once again, God stepped in and one of the greatest blessings from God came into my life.

I did my best to make my marriage work because I now had a son with him and wanted desperately for my little boy to have a father. I did not want to go through another divorce and feel like a failure twice. I tried to be the best wife I could be and sometimes it worked but other times, when he had been out with other women, he would come home angry and start yelling at me. I could not figure out why. The constant stress began affecting my three-year-old son.

Several years before, I had asked God to forgive me for walking away and had asked if He really loved me to show that love to me. I remember where I was driving when a tangible presence of God came into the car and I was enveloped by such a sense of God's love for me that I began to cry to the point where I could hardly drive the car. That love carried me through many tough times during that second marriage and made me turn to God and really seek Him for answers. I finally concluded that I needed to leave that marriage in order to protect my son from the emotional damages.

It was one of the hardest and most painful decisions I had ever made. I had questioned my ex about his infidelity on several occasions, but he had always blamed me for not being trusting enough. He would even turn the tables and say "you must be cheating to even have a thought like that." I knew I was not and would not want to be accused so I quit asking him. After all, that was what a wife was meant to do-believe the best in her husband.

The anger though became so great and his drug use increased. I was concerned for the safety of my son and so I left, thinking that if I did maybe my husband would miss us so much he would agree to go to counseling and change his ways. He did agree to go to counseling, but I found out later he was living with one of his girlfriends during that time. Six months after I left him, he begged me to come back and I was seriously considering it.

In a lot of ways, life was overwhelming. I was renting a new house that was small and needed a lot of repairs plus I was putting in 15 hours at work and had to take my 3 1/2-

year-old with me. I couldn't help but think of the nice home near the beach I had left and the comforts of home, and was wondering if things could work out if I went back. I remember very clearly asking God to give me a sign if I should pack up and move back. Then out of the blue, I got a call asking for my husband. I told the person on the other end this was my number and that my husband and I were separated, and the person said "oh my, I need to tell you something!"

That person then began to unload everything they had seen and heard for the past six years of my marriage. They had worked with my husband and the stories they told of other women suddenly made everything make sense. They intercepted letters with proof of his infidelity and offered to show them to me. I literally felt like someone had punched me in the gut and knocked the wind right out of me. The person I had stood by during some of the worst times in his life, who I wrongly assumed would be loyal because of it, had betrayed me. He did it not once but over and over again from the very beginning of our marriage.

THE SECRET POWER OF FORGIVENESS

I was once again shattered and yet had to somehow pick myself up and go on because I had a little boy to support. That was when I realized God had answered my prayer and showed me very clearly, I was not to go back. Not wanting my son to get pulled into that lifestyle or be around drugs, I went through the process of filing for divorce and getting custody.

Chapter 3: The Darkest Days of My Life

While all this was happening, I was working as Executive Director at a daycare operated by my father's ministry. When they had asked me to come to work, they only had seventeen children and were thinking they were going to have to close due to overhead cost.

I got there, started marketing, and met parents that were looking for a great place to put their kids and began to help transform the daycare into a place, I would want my son to be in. It meant working long hours. We would get there before 6:00 AM and work until well after 6:00 PM.

However, the daycare started growing and the best part was that I was able to have my son there with me as I worked. We grew from having seventeen to almost 80 students in a short time.

I had great relationships with the parents at the daycare and spent many hours praying with them and helping them with some type of crisis they were going through. Most of the time that meant me having to stay late to finish up my work, but the door was always open to parents needing counseling or prayer. Having gone through so much pain myself and knowing what it felt like to need someone to turn to, I wanted to make sure to show them God's love.

We had back-to-school bashes where over the course of three years, we were able to help over 1,500 kids from the community go back with physicals, backpacks, and school supplies. We were feeding children daily who didn't get food at home and I loved knowing we were making such a difference in their lives. We had just received a letter of accommodation from the Department of Children and Family, saying we were the best daycare around the Summerfield, Florida area and had passed all our inspections with flying colors.

Unfortunately, we also faced a lot of challenges, including with personnel. We started noticing that supplies and money were going missing. One girl in particular, who worked in the front office, seemed to be suddenly doing a lot better. She got a new car and moved to a new house. She was the one who helped to take the payments from the parents. I had begun to suspect this woman of misappropriating funds.

We also started noticing the parents were not paying money they owed, yet when asked about the payments, they said they had paid but mysteriously didn't have a receipt. We were so busy and growing so fast that it was hard to keep track of everything.

I found out the girl who worked in the front office began to tell people the school was going to close. I couldn't figure out why on earth she would say that when we were growing, and things seemed to be going so well. We didn't realize it but she was forming a plan to not only make sure we closed but also to destroy many lives in the process.

THE SECRET POWER OF FORGIVENESS

At the time, I just assumed because the economy was bad and schools were closing all around us she was just concerned about that. She was in an abusive marriage and I went out of my way to help her and many of the staff with challenges they were facing. I constantly tried to help them, even by loaning them my own money during times when they said things were too tough.

In addition to everything else, the girl in the front office resented the male teacher we had. She kept saying she thought he was shown favoritism and was very angry because she thought he got preferential treatment. This teacher had a great big heart and was wonderful with the kids. What she didn't realize was that he would leave early a lot of times because he had to go work on songs for church on Sunday because he was the worship leader. As a result, he worked many long nights.

Because of her hatred towards this teacher, she decided to use a very troubled student who had been in our daycare and graduated from pre-kindergarten. He was from a family where both his parents were extremely young. He had caused the school so much trouble that we had to call the parents numerous times.

We caught this boy more times than I could count stealing toys and things from the daycare. He had been sent to the principal's office often for disrupting class. We concluded that he had some major emotional and behavioral issues. He was expelled from two other public schools for the same reason. His parents had begged us to give him a chance, because we really wanted to help them and the boy so we agreed to let him join our kindergarten program.

The whole thing was a recipe for disaster; with the school growing so fast and trying to help so many parents, we didn't see at the time the catastrophe looming on the horizon. The employee that was embezzling money and school supplies knew we were getting suspicious of her activities and decided to make her move using that little boy. She had him make a false allegation against the teacher she didn't like. She then came up to me, telling me that the boy had something to say and that his mother wanted to talk to me also.

THE SECRET POWER OF FORGIVENESS

I sat down with the mother, who told me what her son had said that the "teacher had asked him to touch him inappropriately." I asked where this had taken place and she said that none of them knew. Then I asked her if she would like to confront the teacher in question and she refused. I then asked her if she wanted to take further action. She again refused, saying that nothing happened because "my son said he only asked, and I don't want it to go any further."

Before I could decide what to do, the employee who had instigated the whole thing had contacted a sheriff's detective. I was out of the school at a meeting when I got a call from the office next door asking me if I knew there was a detective in my school. I replied that I did not know, and I immediately hung up and called the school. The employee answered and when I asked what the detective was doing, she lied and said, "I have no idea; let me check and call you back." I replied, "No, put her on the phone now." When the detective got on the phone I got the shock of my life. Little did I know my world was fixing to come crashing down in ways I could never have imagined.

THE SECRET POWER OF FORGIVENESS

The first words out of the detective's mouth were "This is detective ___. I just finished interviewing your son." I said, "Well first off, who gave you permission to even be in the school much less interview my son?" She replied that she would stop until I got there and then revealed that the employee, I had just spoken with had given her my five-year old son to interview.

I called my father who was the president of the whole organization, and asked him to meet me at the school. Both of us were totally unprepared for what we were about to face. When we walked in the door, we were met by the detective. She appeared friendly and since we had never been in trouble with the law and had nothing to hide, we agreed to comply with her without hesitation.

We were questioned for several hours and allowed to hear the tape of the interview with my son, which by the way, was illegally obtained. On that tape he told her he had never seen anything and didn't believe anything had happened. She then asked if she could interview the other kids in the school. As a parent whose son's rights had just been violated, I respectfully said I would be happy to call the parents and if they agreed to the interview, then she could, but the parents needed to give their consent. She said, 'No, then don't worry about it" and concluded the interview saying, "I don't think the teacher acted inappropriately or else I would be arresting him." She then thanked us and said we would probably hear something back in a couple of weeks regarding dropping the whole issue.

That night I tried to do damage control with my son who was scared of the whole situation. He told me the detective had a gun and took him in a room alone to ask him questions about one of his favorite teachers. He told me that he told her the truth that nothing had happened. He said that she kept telling him if he lied to her, he could go to jail and that she seemed to not believe him.

Two days later, I was getting ready for a six-week parenting class we had been advertising. It was the second time we had offered that class. The Department of Children and Families had sent families to us in the past who had to complete classes in order to get custody of their kids. I was thinking about the parents who we had helped before.

Several had completed the six-week class and had gotten their families back together.

I was jolted out of my thoughts by the phone ringing and once again, it was the school calling telling me the Department of Children and Families was in the school and I needed to come quick. I was surprised because although we were contracted with them, usually they showed up for inspections during school hours and the after-hours parenting class was about to start.

I walked in once again unprepared for what was I was going to face. The detective was there once again and was demanding that DCF employees give her our school files including the teachers, students, and anything else she wanted. They complied with her request, although she did not have a warrant and they did not have the legal rights to give the files to her.

She began shouting at me when I walked in the door to show them where the files were and to make copies of those files. I asked her why the change in attitude from a couple of days before and she just continued to scream at me that I was a liar. While I was making copies and

THE SECRET POWER OF FORGIVENESS

shaking like a leaf trying to figure out what was going on, she continued to yell at me and order DCF to get her all of our files.

In the meantime, people were starting to come into the church where the school was and where the parenting class was being held. My father, who was there by this time, had to stop them from coming in the door of the church. They began mingling about in the parking lot wondering what in the world had happened. Then another cop car showed up with lights flashing. He got out and walked into the church.

Up until that time, I had always been told a church was a safe haven and that armed cops could not come in unless invited. I found out pretty quickly that night that a lot of what I had believed regarding law enforcement was not true, especially when we had a rogue detective hell-bent on proving us guilty of this crime because she was trying to make a name for herself.

When we asked what the other cop was doing there, the detective said, "I called him for back up." Then she gave me a paper saying she had the right to take my five-year-old son in for questioning. I immediately asked for an attorney and she said "No, you don't get one! This isn't about you. It is about your son." I said, "Then I want one for him," and she said, "Well he is a minor and doesn't get one either." I figured out right then why they had waited till 6 p.m. to arrive because they knew offices were closed and it would be hard for me to reach an attorney at that hour.

I asked her why she was doing this and from clear across the church, she screamed at me, "Because you hindered the investigation when you stopped me from questioning the other kids. Your son would not be going through this if you had not done that." I said, "Well, you already interviewed my son without my permission, and he told you that nothing had happened."

She then demanded I bring my son, who was with my mother. She was, standing by me fully armed with another cop beside her, yelling aggressively and I was desperately trying to figure out what to do.

A battle was going on in my mind. My mother's instinct was in full gear and what I wanted to do was tell my mother to take him and protect him until I could get an attorney and find out what was going on. The other part of me knew she would arrest me on the spot. I was prepared for that, but I was concerned they would then get my son and put him in DCF custody where he might be further interrogated and traumatized.

I picked up my mobile flip phone to call my mom and planned to speak in another language so the detective could not understand what I was saying. The phone rang a couple of times and then my mother answered. Before I could say anything other than "hi", the detective jerked the phone out of my hand, slammed it shut and said, "You say one word to her other than 'bring my son here' and I will make sure you never see your son again."

At that point, shaken and scared of losing my son and feeling like someone was about to kidnap my baby, I had a decision to make and had to make it instantly. That decision was one I have replayed thousands of times in my mind. I didn't think my mom could have gotten him away safely or I would have told her to run with him. I was afraid the detective would call out a manhunt for them and I would have been in jail, not being able to help them at all.

The order the detective handed me was signed by a judge. The detective had sworn under oath that she had been denied access to my son while thinking he was in danger. The document also gave her permission to take him for questioning. She had clearly lied to get that order. She was brazen enough to come into church, shut down the services and bring armed police back-up to help her while ordering DCF to give her our school documents illegally without a warrant.

At that point, I didn't put anything past her and fully believed her when she said I would never see my son again, so I made the only choice I thought I could. The only thing I knew to do to protect my son was to try my best to cooperate with her. I did not want to make the situation worse than it already was.

I asked my mother to bring my son to the church/school and then begged DCF to please protect him from the detective, who clearly had her own agenda. As I handed my son over to them, I felt like my heart had been ripped out of my chest and all I could do for the next few hours was beg God to protect him and pray they would bring him back.

They finally brought him back 2 1/2 hours later but he was not the same little boy who had left me earlier. Instead, he was a broken shell of my five-year-old, once vibrant son. They had so violently interrogated him mentally and emotionally by exposing him to things he had no clue about. They had stolen his innocence that night in horrific ways that could never be undone. When they handed him back, he literally clung to me saying "Mommy they tried to make me say things that were not true and lie, and when I told them it wasn't true they told me I was lying."

Right away he began to experience post-traumatic stress and was in complete terror. I had no clue what the detective would try again, so I called my sister -in- law. She is an ER nurse and I asked her if she would come get him and take him out of state to live with her and my brother for a while to keep my son safe. She and my brother agreed and she flew down the next day. I met her with my son and together they flew back to Colorado, with me not having a clue when I would see him again. That picture of my shattered little boy who was brave enough to tell the truth, looking back at me as my sister- in- law took him to board the plane, is one I will never get out of my mind.

I have experienced much heartache in my life but the worst thing I have ever experienced was watching my son suffer and not being able to help him. Sending him away to protect him just about killed me. I was sobbing so hard as I left the airport that I could hardly see to drive. If you would have taken everything I had ever gone though in my life up until that point and weighed it next to the trauma we went through that week and the months to come, it would not have even come close.

Over the next few months, the detective did her best to arrest me and my father. She monitored our every move including listening to phone calls, following us, and trying to find out if we were hindering her investigation in anyway. We learned that the concept of "innocent until proven guilty" was another false belief we had held. She put a gag order on us and said if we said one word to

THE SECRET POWER OF FORGIVENESS

anyone we would be arrested. She went around the neighborhood by the church and publicly told everyone that abuse had been going on for a year and half and we did nothing to stop it. Then, when we were asked to comment we couldn't respond, or she said she would arrest us.

She eventually got a young man to go along with her story of abuse. He was no longer even at our school and had only attended the after-school program briefly. His mother had to pull him out because of lack of funds, and he was so upset to have to leave. However, he agreed to testify against the teacher but then later he told several people he had made everything up to get attention. The detective did arrest the teacher on trumped up charges, five of which she said were from my son, who again had told her nothing ever happened.

I learned way more about the corruption of the judicial system than I ever wanted to know. The detective called us and all the teachers that worked for the daycare to be deposed and made us sit for hours in the sheriff's department. She then aggressively questioned each of us separately for hours, trying to trip us up in some way.

THE SECRET POWER OF FORGIVENESS

The detective eventually did get one of the teachers who had recently been dismissed for failure to show up to work and lying about it, to cooperate with her. Shockingly enough, that teacher and her husband had both been very good friends with the teacher who was accused.

In fact, under oath, her husband had said he had never ever witnessed anything inappropriate and that he knew the teacher in question was not capable of such crimes. However, his wife agreed to lie and gave a testimony contrary to his, so he went back and changed his story to protect his wife from perjury. They both began to spy on us and the church, and when we would ask for prayer for the accused teacher, they would report it to the detective. The detective even went to court and tried to get another order to have all the church bulletins, emails, texts and any other personal documentation or communication turned over to her. Fortunately, this time the judge ruled that it was an invasion of privacy.

Over the next couple of years, we continued to battle her injustice. For a year I would fly to Colorado once a month to spend a week with my son. He was in counseling to get help emotionally and mentally. Each time I left Colorado, my heart felt like it was ripped out of my chest, but with work and the investigation going on, I had to go back to Florida. I wanted to bring him back with me, but the counselor told me his trauma was so severe that he couldn't return to that area for a while.

We eventually got the DVD's from all the kids the detective had interviewed and found out they had not treated any of the other kids the way they interrogated my son. The parents of all the other kids were allowed to be with them when they were questioned. In the interviews, the children were coached to agree with the allegations by leading questions such as "So where did he touch you?" or "When he touched you, where was it?" Instead of the kids (who ranged in age from three to five years-old) agreeing with the allegations, they gave raving reviews about what a great teacher he was and how much they liked him. I watched the DVD of the interviews with the other children. I saw her say to the parents, "Wendy really should be telling you what is going on here at the school. Has she said, "anything to you at all?" When they would say "no," she would say, "are you sure, that is shocking that she would be such a coward as to not tell you the truth about what is happening?"

Nevertheless, the detective insisted on continuing the investigation and continued to terrorize us. She often checked in with the parents to see if I had said anything to them about what was going on. She was trying to see if I did so she could arrest me.

By that time, we had an attorney who had warned me that the detective was on a witch hunt and that we needed to not say anything to anyone about what was going on. It was so hard to not be able to tell the parents of the students the truth of what had happened. I wanted to tell them about what had been done to my son. I wanted to tell them that I did not want their children to be subjected to that. I wanted to tell them that we had been threatened that if my father or I spoke to anyone, we would be arrested.

I knew if I could have just told them the truth it would have given them peace of mind. I had protected their kids from being brutally interrogated like my son was. The detective knew that also so she made sure that we couldn't even respond to the TV crews and newspaper reporters that were showing up outside of our church and homes asking questions.

The community thought we were guilty. The parents didn't know the truth and were very angry that I was not talking. They were being told that I knew abuse was going on and had allowed it for over a year so they begin to take their anger and frustrations out on me.

Parents started withdrawing their kids from the daycare. Others started trashing our church property, while other went on social media to slander us. I got more phone calls than I could count of people screaming at me and all the while, I couldn't say anything other than "I am sorry." Even those very ones I had helped the most through challenges with DCF concerning their own kids, began to harshly criticize us.

We had one meeting where our attorney was going to speak to the parents. That meeting was on the same day the detective called us in for questioning and had made all of us sit in her office for well over eight hours, questioning and accusing all of us of lying. She also made sure to give an interview to the newspaper that came out that same day we were being interrogated. She did not have proof of any of the nineteen trumped up charges but her interview with the newspaper, she spoke as though they were facts.

She didn't even allege that it had happened but instead said, "While the teacher has been singing God's praises, he actually has been doing the devil's work behind closed doors and the pastor and his daughter have known about it and covered up for over a year and a half."

That night as I sat on the front pew of the church, my father on one side of the church and me on the other, I was broken-hearted because I could not talk. I knew that if I could talk, it would clear up the whole situation. I was thinking of all the parents I had helped over the past couple of years, of all the fun VPK graduations we had celebrated and the Christmas programs where the church was packed with people driving from as far away as Georgia.

I remembered the parents who had spent hours in my office sharing the heartache they were going through. We had cried together, laughed together, prayed together, and after all the things I had done to help them, I was now the enemy in their eyes. I knew that many were hurt and confused. Yet I was the only one whose son had been emotionally and psychologically abused, not by the teacher but by law enforcement. Not only was I prohibited from relaying the truth to people I once considered friends, but I was also grieving in being apart from my son.

I wanted to stand up and scream "You all know me; I would have done anything to protect your kids and I did! I treated them the way I would want my child to be treated and your children were not abused. This is a vicious witch hunt and if your child was abused, I would be the first one to make sure someone paid for it." Instead, I had to sit there alone, and devastated as parent after parent got up at the meeting and screamed, "How could you let this happen?"

One couple, who didn't even have their kids enrolled and had left months earlier owing us lots of money, went screaming out of the church, dropping the F-bomb as they left. Another woman whose grandson I had helped when the family went through challenging times, stood up and told lies. I just looked at her through tears and shock knowing she knew she was lying but also knowing, at that point, everyone was so angry and hurt by the lies the detective had told them that they were just becoming an angry mob.

Only one lady in the whole church stood up in defense of me and said, "I know these people; they are good, and they would not allow something like this. There must be something they can't say." I wanted to hug her that night and to this day for her bravery.

Many of the teachers, who we had to let go because the school had dropped from almost eighty students down to twenty, flipped and began to say mean things about us and the school although none could truthfully say there had been abuse of any kind. One of them actually called the same detective who had interrogated my son and told her, "Wendy just threw her son away like a piece of trash and sent him to Colorado if you need to get him again." When I heard that recorded phone call later, I couldn't believe a person could be so heartless, especially one who we had helped in her own abusive marriage and with her own kids more times than I can count.

After two horrible long years of nonstop legal battles, investigations, and dealing with a corrupt justice system, we came to understand that the accused teacher could not get a fair trial. He didn't have the money for a good attorney, so we helped him through fundraising, but our involvement made us look suspicious and didn't help his case.

He also still needed help paying for expert witnesses. It was frustrating that although he was entitled to a fair trial the state refused to advocate for his case or provide him with any means to conduct a fair trial. There was literally no way for him to rightly defend himself. We were out of funds because we had to still pay all the teachers after many of the parents had left without paying what they owed us.

I went to the State Attorney's office, who was calling my son as a witness, and brought them a letter from the Christian counselor he had been seeing, telling them that it would be detrimental to my son to put him on a stand at seven years of age, after all they had already put him through. The counselor had said in the letter that there were no signs that he had been abused by the teacher in any way, but there were huge signs that indicated the detective had traumatized him with the investigation.

I will never forget what the state attorney prosecuting the case said to me that day. He said "First, I don't care what your paper says. If I want to put your son on a stand, I will do it. Second, I don't care if the teacher did it or didn't do, I will still prosecute him."

A few months later, they offered to drop all charges except for one if the teacher would agree to plead no contest. Otherwise, they were going to give him 60 years for each of the 19 false charges. If he would plead no contest, they would give him 10 years' probation. It was clear that with a mob mentality and us not being able to come out with the whole truth or more money he wouldn't get a fair trial, so he took the deal.

Once again, my heart was broken. I felt like I had failed this teacher in some way by not being able to protect him. He never deserved to be accused and treated like that. He had spent three months in jail and had not ever been in trouble with the law before this. The whole time he was there, I was up many nights praying for him. He was great

THE SECRET POWER OF FORGIVENESS

with the kids and had a real gift of being patient and kind with them when others would be frustrated. He also had fantastic talents for helping with plays and leading worship. He was always willing to lend a helping hand with anything the church needed. As part of his condition of probation he could no longer be anywhere around us. The injustice he went through is still hard to comprehend.

Those years were, without a doubt, some of the darkest days of my life. I remember month after month flying back from Colorado to Florida and having to leave my son behind. He would cling to me and beg me not to go and as desperately as I didn't want to, I had no choice. I had to keep things going with work and be there in case my father got arrested, but of course my son was too young to understand. I wanted to bring him home with me but his counselor thought it was best he didn't go back. He had been having nightmares since the incident and we couldn't shake him out of it. He also began to try and get himself out of ropes he would tie in knots in case they arrested him so he could learn to escape. If he saw police car or police, he would have a complete panic attack. He had gone from a very outgoing boy to one that was terrified to be around people or loud noises.

People he thought he could trust, police officers, were the very ones who had terrorized him so his whole world was shaken and worse yet, they had told him I was the reason he went through it all. When he told them nothing had happened and the teacher had never done anything to him they said "well, your mother told us he did so why are you lying." He went through that for hours and yet still kept telling them the truth and refused to lie. But it made him feel as if there was no one, including his mother, who could protect him.

I would be lying if I told you I didn't want to hurt the detective for taking my child's innocence. There is a tape that shows the several hours of interrogation he endured. I didn't and couldn't watch it because I was warned by a few others that it was brutal and they didn't stop badgering him even when he put his head down and sobbed begging for his mother and asking to go home.

I saw the Detective as someone who was pure evil who had literally come into the church and kidnapped my son,

THE SECRET POWER OF FORGIVENESS

although not at gun point, she did have a gun and another officer with one and threatened me if I didn't do what she said I would never see my son again. I found out later she couldn't have done that except that she lied under oath to the judge. I also found out later she had brutalized many people including other churches while she worked at the Sheriff's Department.

Later, under deposition, the detective lied repeatedly to our attorney. Our attorney finally stopped questioning her because it was evident that she was not going to be truthful.

I went to the Sheriff's Department and asked them to investigate her. They said they would look into it but did nothing. I then went to the State Attorney's office and asked them to press charges for what she had done to my son and for perjury and they said "If the Sheriff's Department wants us to, we will." There was a good 'ole boy system that ran so deep that not even attorneys would take the case for fear of what would happen to them. It wasn't until years later that we found out the reason they came after us with such a vengeance.

Evidently there was someone who had run a school who actually did abuse kids and who should have been arrested but they had dropped the ball on him so he had gotten away and gone to other states and repeated the offense.

As a result, there was state funding up for grabs to whoever (the Department of Children & Families or the Sheriff's Department) could get a case, take it to trial and win. That agency would get the state funding worth millions of dollars so we just happened to be the ones they went after. It was a direct attack of the enemy because we were doing so much to help the children of our community and they thought that would also make a bigger case when we went to trial.

I was so hurt, broken, angry, and spent many sleepless nights worrying about the children that had been at our daycare. Some of them had not had food at home and we made sure that they had at least two good meals and snacks while they were with us. In my mind, that detective and the Sheriff's Department had not only mentally and emotionally abused my son but also stopped me from making sure the children of the community were fed and well taken care of.

The reason I have shared all this from past with you is because I want you to know that when I talk about "The Secret Power of Forgiveness," I know firsthand what I am talking about. Through immense injustice, betray and heartache I have had to make a deliberate choice to forgive so many people that I didn't think I could forgive at that time. Anyone that has been involved in ministry for a long time will tell you that often the ones that hurt and slander you the most are the very ones you have invested in and helped the most. The challenge of working with people is many are hurting and broken themselves and hurting people hurt people.

So, when I tell you I understand firsthand how hard it can be to forgive, I truly do understand. These things that I have shared here are just a drop in the bucket of many injustices and betrays I have experienced over the years.

Yet, I can also honestly tell you that everything I have shared with you I have done without malice or bitterness or unforgiveness. I couldn't always say that, especially right when it was all happening, but I have learned over the years that forgiveness is the only way to be free. It is the only way to not be tied to the very ones who tried to destroy you.

It is the only way to live a life that is not filled with bitterness and regret. Even beyond that, it is the only way to not become like the very people who hurt you.

I know some of you may still have your doubts about the value of forgiveness or even if you can do it. I am going to share some secrets so you too can come to understand the secret power that comes with forgiveness.

Chapter 4: Discovering What Forgiveness Really Is

Before we can really talk about forgiveness, we need to know what forgiveness is and what it isn't. I think the reason so many people struggle with forgiveness is because they have a false concept of what it means.

Forgiveness does *not* mean letting a person off the hook or pretending that what they did was okay. It doesn't mean that what you went through was not a real hurt or that you shouldn't be upset by what someone did to you.

Forgiveness isn't about putting yourself back into a situation that is harmful. It isn't about negating what happened in any way. Forgiveness isn't about letting them off of the hook. It is about letting yourself off the hook.

THE SECRET POWER OF FORGIVENESS

Forgiveness isn't a feeling, it's a deliberate and sometimes minute by minute choice. Eventually the feeling of forgiveness will come but not necessarily the moment you choose to forgive. Some people say they are going to forgive. However, the moment they don't feel the warm fuzzy feelings for the individual that wronged them, they think they haven't forgiven and are waiting on those feelings to forgive.

There has been so much confusion about forgiveness for so long that people just give up. Many say, "I just can't forgive" as if them not forgiving is going to somehow punish the person that wronged them. But forgiveness is not just for the other person, it is for you. You see, if we don't forgive, we are forever tied to the person who wronged us. I have watched people over the years who refuse to forgive someone become bitter, angry, and eventually all they can focus on in life is the person that wronged them. One single person who hurt them has sucked the joy out of their whole life and stopped them from truly living because all they focus on and talk about is the hurt they experienced and how much they despise that individual. Many times, the person that hurt them has gone on living their life and doesn't care or remember what was done. However, the hurting individual eventually starts to look like the very one that hurt them. Its almost as if they become a mirror image of the person that wronged them. Often the same character flaws they despise in that individual they begin to demonstrate to others as well. I was fascinated by this. So, I begin to ask God. Why, when someone refused to forgive many times, they not only resembled in action but sometimes even in facial expressions the very person they hated the most?

God gave me a visual that made me decide right then and there that no matter what I walked through; I must choose forgiveness. He showed me that when we are formed in our mothers' womb, we have an umbilical cord that ties us to them. Everything that our mothers eat, drink, or take during that pregnancy comes through the umbilical cord and affects our development.

In the same way, when someone does something to hurt us, there is a spiritual cord that connects us to that individual. The only way that we can prevent their influence from flowing into us is by making a deliberate choice to forgive and cut the cord. If we don't forgive, we are literally tied to them in the spirit and everything in them (all the hate, bitterness, and evil) flows from them into us. It affects every area of our lives, and will bind us to them tighter and tighter until we choose to cut the cord and walk free.

Choosing forgiveness is saying "God, I am choosing as an act of my will to cut this cord tying me to this individual." If you can picture a cord connected to you and to the individual that wronged, you. Then visualize yourself cutting it in the middle. So, your cord is still connected to you and theirs is still connected to them but now you are no longer joined by that cord. Then you make a choice to give God the cord connected to you. That allows God to begin to flow into your life with His healing power and His Spirit can begin to flow in your life and remove the pain and hurt you have experienced. When you release all ties and anger from this individual, God can then take what you've been through and begin to work it out for your good.

THE SECRET POWER OF FORGIVENESS

When you choose to do it God's way, He now has access to begin to pour into you what you need to be able to grow and become all he created you to be in life.

The individual that hurt you illegally came against you in the spirit realm and you did have a legal right to hold them hostage but instead you chose to forgive and do it God's way. You now have a legal right to give their cord that is attached to them to God and say God I now give you legal access into their life to do what you need to do to take care of the situation. God says that vengeance is His and He will repay. He won't let them off the hook but when you do it God's way, it allows Him to actually have direct access to do what He needs to do in their life as well.

One example of the power of forgiveness in the Bible can be found in Acts 7. There was a man named Saul who had been killing Christians, He was doing everything in his power to track them down, torture, and destroy them. He was hell bent on annihilating anyone who got in his way. In Acts 7 it tells us that Paul was holding the coats of men as they were stoning a godly man named Stephen.

Stephen had done nothing wrong other than he loved Jesus and Saul an extremely religious man hated him for it. He eventually had Stephen captured and stood there watching as others stoned him to death. The Bible tells us that as this was happening, Stephen looked up into heaven and he chose forgiveness. He cut the cord that tied him to the people who were killing him and he gave it to God asking God to forgive them as well.

Did these people deserve to pay for what they were doing to Stephen? Absolutely! Would Stephen have been justified in his anger toward them? Yes! He could have and no one would have blamed him, but God's ways are not our ways, and God knows the best way for us to be free from the pain and hurt we have walked through.

In Stephen's case, the way to be free was for God to just take him out of there altogether and get him to Heaven. Meanwhile, God was also moving in Saul's life. In the very next chapter you see Saul on his way to kill more Christians, but he gets knocked right off his donkey and blinded by God, unable to go any further until he was willing to repent and beg God for mercy. I have often thought about all the Christians that Saul might have continued to kill had Stephen not chosen forgiveness and to do it God's way.

Stephen isn't the only one in the Bible that did that, though. You see, Stephen was also once in need of forgiveness, like others who have sinned. God knew this and provided a way for people to be saved by also forgiving them. To do so, Jesus hung on the cross and went through untold agony to pay the price for our sin.

Jesus was perfect and had never done any wrong. He didn't have to go to the cross but He He chose to do it God's way so that we might receive forgiveness. Jesus had the right to not forgive. He had been done wrong by the very people He had helped the most; people He had loved, healed, fed, cared for, and spent time with. Yet they betrayed him and had him killed. Jesus had every reason to be angry and bitter and to ask God to condemn them all to hell. But instead, the final thing He did was ask God to forgive them. Even in the garden of Gethsemane, Jesus was asking God if there was any other way to avoid all the pain and suffering He was about to go through. But He loved us so much that He did it anyway. That allowed God legal access into all our lives and took back the power from the enemy and gave it back to God. That is why the Bible says in 1 John 1:9 KJV, "If we confess our sin, He is faithful and just to forgive our sin." We don't deserve it but Jesus chose forgiveness so we can receive God's forgiveness in our lives.

Thankfully, Stephen, also chose forgiveness which stopped Saul from killing many more Christians. Because he did God was able to give Saul a whole new identity and even changed his name from Saul to Paul. Paul still had to pay for what he had done. He still had consequences and endured a lot of what he had put the Christians he had persecuted through, although now instead of harming them, he joined them and became even more vocal about God's love. He then lived on as a fierce warrior for God and wrote over 1/3 of the New Testament.

Again, think about what would have happened if Stephen wouldn't have chosen forgiveness? Stephen made a decision that impacted generations of people even down to today. His forgiveness acted as a catalyst to re-work

THE SECRET POWER OF FORGIVENESS

Saul's heart and turn it for good. When you choose forgiveness, God gets involved on your behalf and He will take care of them and deal with them.

The act of forgiveness can not only change your life but the person that hurt you. We must remember that God loves all His children, even the ones whose sin seems more apparent/visible. However, I have also seen God deal with people in ways that I ended up feeling sorry for the very ones that wronged me. The Bible is very clear God is a God of justice. He is our Father and He doesn't want to see one of His children hurt. You may think by choosing forgiveness you are allowing that person off the hook for what they did. Instead it allows God to take care of it on your behalf, and many times in the process radically impacts their lives as well.

Forgiveness is an act of your will just like getting up and going to work when you would rather stay in bed is an act of your will. You chose to do it in spite of how you are feeling because you want to reap the benefit of getting paid and having food and shelter. That is the same thing with forgiveness; you make a deliberate choice to say "Father, I choose, as an act of my will, to forgive ---------------. I cut the spiritual umbilical cord and I give my end to you so you can begin to heal me of all the hurt and pain that I have gone through. I also chose to give you the cord that was connected to them and ask that you do what you need to in their life.

Making that chose to forgive may be something you literally have to do minute by minute depending on what you have been through. The thing that will help motivate you to make that choice is knowing there are some major benefits to you as you do.

Chapter 5: Forgive for The Health of It

When you choose not to forgive, it is extremely detrimental to your wellbeing, both spiritually and physically. There is a verse in the Bible that says "Be angry, and do not sin": do not let the sun go down on your wrath,."NKJ I always thought that was because you are supposed to just start afresh the next day. However, there is also a legitimate health reason for it. When you go to bed angry each night, it begins to stop the feel-good hormone, serotonin, from being produced in your body. Serotonin is the hormone that is released when you eat carbs. It gives you a sense of wellbeing and makes you feel happy. When you go to bed mad each night, your body stops producing that hormone and makes you feel restless. It then starts a chain reaction from being merely restless, to being angry/hateful, and ultimately causing you more pain than you anticipated/intended and can lead to depression.

One statistic shows that 1 in 10 people in America are on antidepressant medicines. When I worked as an assessment counselor at a major psychiatric hospital, I saw many people dealing with depression. The hospital would admit them and keep them for 30 days. They would put them on antidepressants, and then send them home. But 30 days later, they would be back again even more depressed than before. Instead of treating the root cause, they simply tried to mask the symptoms with temporary solutions and the people just continued to deteriorate. I found it so disheartening especially because it appeared to be only about how much money that the hospital and doctors could make, instead of helping the patient.

God has a lot of natural/holistic solutions He provides and one of the most effective ones is forgiveness. If we do not follow His advice, we see all kinds of consequences manifest in our physical body.

Many Dr's will tell you chronic anger puts you into a fight-or-flight mode, which results in numerous changes in heart rate, blood pressure, and decreases your immune response. As a result that will lead to, an increase the risk of depression, heart disease, and diabetes, among many other conditions.

Another study shows that unforgiveness is classified in medical journals as an actual disease.

Of all cancer patients, 61% have forgiveness issues, and of those, more than half are severe, according to research. Holding on to negative emotions, anger, hatred, and bitterness creates a state of chronic anxiety.

Chronic anxiety will produce excess adrenaline and cortisol, which deplete the production of natural killer cells, which is your body's foot soldier in the fight against cancer. Holding onto anger, even for a legitimate reason, leads to bitterness and may cause adverse changes in metabolism, immune system function, and organ function. It can also put our minds on a never-ending loop of replaying the event over and over again. That will only lead to downward spiral into an abyss that will be extremely challenging to climb out of. If you want to learn more about how our bodies do or don't function based on our thinking, I encourage you to get ahold of Dr. Caroline Leaf's books. Dr. Leaf is a Cognitive Neuroscientist that shows the links between science and what God has to say about us. She will give you tangible tools to help control your thoughts and emotions which will lead to a vastly improved lifestyle.

Also there are many nutritional products that can support your body when you have gone through a lot of emotional trauma sometimes you deplete your body of vital nutrients that can make it hard to cope much less overcome depression. Finding a good Dr who specializes in health and nutrition can be a key in helping to support you physically as you work through the challenges of forgiveness.

Another issue with refusing to forgive is that it can lead to addiction. You see, when we refuse to deal with the anger and hurt, we are feeling, we tend to want to push them down. Rather than feel the pain often people chose drugs, alcohol, or food to literally drown their sorrows.

Bars all around the world are filled with broken and hurting people who have not chosen forgiveness and instead, are trying to numb the pain by having one more drink or high to avoid dealing with a very real need to heal the hurt in their lives.

Instead of that being a solution, it only aids in furthering the pain through even more dangerous choices that oftentimes leads to even more hurt and brokenness and so begins a vicious cycle on a never ending roller coaster ride of pain and heartbreak. They try to find the solution for the wrong that has been done to them at the bottom of the glass or by getting high enough to temporary forget the pain. The trouble with that is, eventually they have to come crashing down only to find the memories still there waiting to be dealt with although the person that did them wrong, has long since moved on.

Sadly, another thing people use to numb the pain they are in is food. A lot of times people who have had some form of sexual abuse or assault often use food to help suppress and insolate them from the pain. They can struggle with bulimia, anorexia or binge eating. Since they couldn't control the abuse they went through and feel the need to control something, often times food becomes something that can help mask the pain or bring momentary comfort in some way and serve to help them feel more in control.

Other times, it literally becomes an insulator to try and protect themselves from the outside world or from experiencing more pain and the more weight they gain, the more of a shield they feel they are putting up. However, the same wall you build to keep others out also keeps you trapped inside.

Cutting oneself is another form of addiction that people use to deal with the anger and bitterness and hurt they are feeling. When they hurt themselves physically, in some way it helps to relieve the emotional pain because the physical pain allows for some distraction from the inward pain they can't find a way to express.

So if you are struggling with addictions or with physical issues, one way to begin to see improvement in those areas is to choose forgiveness and sometimes the person you have to forgive is yourself.

Chapter 6: Letting Yourself Off of The Hook

I found when I started working on forgiveness issues that the first person I had to forgive was me. You see, you can't overcome what you won't confront. For some reason we as humans have a hard time acknowledging areas in our lives that we perceive to be weakness.

We want to blame everyone around us for how we turned out or for why things are a certain way in our lives. We make statements like "Well, if you only knew what they did to me," or "if I hadn't gone through. [fill in the blank] my life would be different." We point fingers at others and focus too much on what we think someone should have done for us or how they should have treated us.

Often using that as an excuse not to deal with our own lives.

The truth is that all of us have gone through challenges in our lives that are unfair, some maybe more than others. The thing is, if we maintain a pitiful attitude, we cannot become powerful. I remember a conversation I had with a friend in my younger days; she told me how rough her life was and I argued by telling her how tough I was having it. She said "yeah, you think that is bad just listen to this." In the middle of her telling me what she was going through was worse, I suddenly realized I didn't want to be more pitiful than her but wanted to make the choice to become powerful.

Sometimes, in our zeal to convince others that we are worse off than them we lose sight of what we really want in our lives. The trouble with unforgiveness is that it causes us to focus on the perceived or very real injustice done to us. That leads us to focus on our anger and bitterness toward the individual that did the wrong and the more we focus on that, the more we allow ourselves to wallow in self-pity and

THE SECRET POWER OF FORGIVENESS

negativity. It is impossible to move forward in life as long as we are focused on the rear-view mirror.

Part of my growth was acknowledging that I needed forgiveness for some of the choices in my life. Taking personal responsibility for the part I played in them took me from being the victim to the victor.

We always have a choice in how we deal with what we go through. We can choose to walk around in chains of despair, forever tied to the horrific event that took place in our lives or we can make a deliberate choice to break those ties and set ourselves free to become all we were created to be. Sometimes that must happen through having someone to talk to, for example, like a family member, trusted friend, or Christian counselor. If we make the right choice, it will empower us to live a life of freedom, not one forever tied to the event we went through.

When we went through the horrific challenges with our daycare, I blamed myself for a long time. I couldn't get out of my mind all the children I knew were going hungry. Or all the people who were so hurt by those events. So many different scenarios played in my head of how I could have prevented it. Or what I could have done to stop it if I had only seen it coming.

I beat myself up more than anyone-for what the teacher who was falsely accused went through and for what my son had to suffer. I would just break down crying uncontrollably. I would think about the corrupt detective, losing friendships with parents and staff, being separated from my son, and the condemnation of an innocent man. I wept, and asked God why he allowed such terrible things to happen.

Yet, through it all, the person I blamed the most was myself. I replayed thoughts like, "If only I had not been so busy, if only I had caught the thief sooner, if only I had followed my instinct instead of letting someone talk me out of firing her when I felt like something was wrong." I felt like I had let down everyone who had put their trust in me, including my son. I wondered why I couldn't have protected them from unseen evil. What could I have done differently? That question played millions of times in my head.

THE SECRET POWER OF FORGIVENESS

Eventually, the only way to begin the healing process was to make a deliberate choice to forgive myself. I am not going to lie and say it was easy. It definitely wasn't! I had to seek a Christian counselor, who helped walk me through the healing process.

Oftentimes, we ourselves are the ones we have the hardest times forgiving. We tend to blame ourselves more than others so, in order to avoid that, we play the blame game and focus our attentions on those other people who did what they did to us. As long as we refuse to acknowledge what happened, we stay stuck in denial and can't reach the next step, which is forgiveness.

Sometimes we need to acknowledge that we are human, and some situations are beyond our control and if we had known better, we would have done better. We can then confront the feelings of "would have," "should have," and "could have" and choose to allow healing to flow even to ourselves for what we think we might could have done differently. Sometimes there wasn't anything we could have done to prevent a situation; we can only control how we respond to it, as well as the choice we make in the future.

THE SECRET POWER OF FORGIVENESS

For example, when I divorced my ex-husband, I worried about my son growing up without a father/in a divided home. I beat myself up for not providing him with the most ideal childhood/living situation, but I had to realize blaming myself would not make things better. Instead, I decided to think about how grateful I was for the gift of my son and I had not made the choices I made he might not have been born. Even when we go through pain because of our own making we need to be willing to choose to forgive ourselves for choices that affected all those around us.

One of those choices that so many people have made is abortion. I mention this subject because sadly, half of the abortions today are by someone who is involved in church. I think it is because people are afraid of the judgment that might come from admitting they are pregnant and think it is a quick fix to just keep people from finding out.

What they are not told at the time of an abortion is that not only will it affect the baby but it will cause both the mom and the dad emotional wounds forever. People pushing abortions want you to think it is a quick fix to a problem you don't want to have to deal with but nothing could be further from the truth. Abortion doesn't end the problem, it begins it. The emotional scars, anger and bitterness that comes long after the baby is gone will continue to destroy your life unless you allow God to forgive you and heal you and also chose to forgive yourself for the choice you made. If you are expecting and feel alone, find a good Christian person and ask them to help guide you through it. There are many organizations that will not only help you emotionally but also assist you financially in being able to keep the baby. Abortion is never the answer and will only cause you more pain.

God promises to work everything, even the hard things, together for our good. He promises in Romans 8:28,NIV "And we know that in all things God works for the good of those who love him, who have been called according to his purpose." While I do not know what you have gone through I do know that God can take the biggest messes and greatest heartaches and bring beauty out of the ashes of our pain.

THE SECRET POWER OF FORGIVENESS

God knows everything about you down to the smallest detail and created you for a unique purpose.

The Bible tells us from the foundations of the earth God knew you and chose you. Ephesians 1:4

Isaiah 43:1 says We do not have to be afraid because He has ransomed us and called us by our name.

These verses mean to say that God knew you and everything that you were going to go through in life; both good and bad. He promised to work even the evil for good if you only allow Him, but it starts with making the choice to ask Him for forgiveness for all the times we have missed the mark and sinned.

If we only accept Jesus' gift of salvation and ask for forgiveness of our sins, He will lead us and guide us into all truth.

Chapter 7: So, What Is the Secret Power in Forgiveness?

Oftentimes on the other side of what looks like the hardest thing we can imagine, having to confront the pain or shame of what we have done or what has been one to us is Freedom!

Yes, forgiveness can feel like an impossible burden to big to bear and confronting it can feel like we are ripping out our very own heart. Yet the truth is on the other side of dealing with the pain by making the deliberate choice to forgive can feel like a huge burden is lifted.

The weight is finally lifted from your shoulders. We can feel free as a bird to soar to new heights as the pain of yesterday no longer weighs us down. It doesn't happen overnight, but the secret is taking the first step by making the choice to forgive.

While I was writing this book, I got a call from a woman who began to share her story. Her husband had run off with her best friend eight years ago and her heart was shattered in a million pieces. She replayed the incident repeatedly to the point where it affected her health, job and every area of her life.

The sad part is, I am sure the couple who broke her heart has long since moved on and although they will pay for their consequences, they are probably not reliving the pain everyday like she is. What they did to her was awful, but what she has allowed to continue is far worse because it has robbed her of joy for the past eight years.

So, the secret is, when you make the choice to forgive, as painful as it may be, it is not nearly as painful as choosing not to forgive. Forgiving saves you from a lot of heartache and from remaining stagnant. It begins your journey to being able to completely walk free of the pain and memories.

THE SECRET POWER OF FORGIVENESS

When I was a little girl living in Papua New Guinea, we had old windows that were glass slats. They required a crank to close them. One day when I was in a hurry, I tried to close them by pushing them with my hand and sliced my hand open. That cut has long since healed but I still have a scar. I can show you where it was cut but when I look at it, I don't feel the pain. Forgiveness is much like that.

Making the choice to forgive can be very painful because we have to look at the situation and deal with it. Sometimes we think that by forgiving someone, we are letting them off the hook but the reality is, the person we are pardoning is ourselves. The person we allow to walk free and no longer carry all the pain is our own self. The secret is that oftentimes on the other side, what looks like our greatest pain is our greatest freedom and victory.

It's like when we were children and we were scared to look under the bed. What if there was a monster under there? When we finally got the courage to look, we found out that what we thought was a monster was just empty space. It can be like that with anything that seems daunting or unknown, and you don't know the outcome until you try.

Don't let the people who hurt you rent space in your life! Make the choice to set yourself free by choosing to cut the spiritual cord that ties you to them and let God begin to fill you up with His love and His healing power in your life.

I told the lady who had been dealing with eight years of pain that you have to make the choice to forgive. Each time that record plays in your head, you must think of the old record players and pick up the needle and move it. Sometimes the old record players would get stuck and go around and around, hitting the same note over and over again. We would have to deliberately get up and move the needle to another spot. It's the same thing with forgiveness once you make the choice. Then the enemy or the inner self begins to remind you of the hurt and pain. You have to say "no, I chose as an act of my will to forgive----------" and then give them to God.

That is what the Bible talks about when it says we are to renew our mind. We have to replace the old way of thinking or like Zig Ziglar, used to say the "stinking

THE SECRET POWER OF FORGIVENESS

thinking" (the old ways of thinking that kept you held down to the pain of your past).

God wants to bring you into total victory so that when you think of what you went through, there is no pain attached to it.

We have to make a choice each time the thought comes back and refuse to focus on the pain of the past, instead replacing it with what we want to see God do in our lives. He can make something beautiful out of what we have been through.

The Bible says, "as a man or woman thinks in his heart so is he." In other words, what you constantly think about, you become or bring about. When you choose forgiveness, also choose to change your thinking and focus on where you are going instead of where you have been.

Chapter 8: Gaining a Right Perspective of God

Maybe you are like me when I was growing up. I had this concept that God was out to get me and just looking for ways to crush me like a bug. I saw Him as this huge, powerful man in the sky who was always waiting for me to mess up and enact judgment on me. Everything bad that happened in my life, I blamed Him thinking He was mad at me for not living up to some unattainable goal that was impossible to reach. Besides, I thought anything that was fun, was sinful so I was pretty certain that He was on a mission to destroy my life.

That perception of God was only made worse by so called "Christians" who claimed to have the most of God yet walked around looking and acting like that just eaten

THE SECRET POWER OF FORGIVENESS

sour grapes. Their self-righteous condemnation only managed to push me even further from God. Because we had lived in so many Pastors homes growing up, I had a bird's eye view of what really went on behind closed doors. Many of them in private were not who the publicly claimed to be in the Pulpit.

One man who was a leader of a huge school admitted to my father that he didn't believe what he preached but he had to preach it or else he would be kicked out of the organization. He couldn't afford the financial loss or job loss so he went along to get along with them even though he didn't believe what he was preaching.

The inconsistencies and pretense, bordering on hypocrisy, that I saw all around me didn't do anything to draw me closer to God, who I felt already couldn't be trusted. What was worse was watching people that I did have confidence in drastically change and shun people that they perceived not to be as holy as they were.

Many times, before my father would speak at a church, we were sent the rules we had to follow before we arrived. Each church had their own manual and set of rules that they expected us to go by while we were with them. I remember one church where the preacher stood up and said that both the Bible and church manual were equal. Yet more often then not I would watch people who swore to go by their church manual break their word when they thought others would not know. It all seemed to be based in fear of pleasing and living up to men's expectations rather then loving God.

Sadly, many times the list of rules was a way of not having to deal with much more sinister things going on behind the scenes, like women and children being abused while everyone looked the other way. They acted like as long as they looked the part outwardly of what they thought a "Christian" should then nothing else really mattered. Many times, they refused to deal with the real heart issues because they were unwilling to confront the truth of sin in their lives. Thankfully after much soul searching and a 40 day fast my Father made the painful but deliberate choice to obey God rather than men's opinion and manmade rules.

Because of the legalism and hypocrisy and the church turning a blind eye, my father felt like God called him to a much higher standard of living than what he was currently seeing in the church. He was to live in such a way that truly reflected the character of Jesus. Instead of following mans' opinion he felt God calling him to totally serve Jesus and truly follow the Bible above anything else. You would have thought his friends would have cheered him on in that endeavor, but nothing could be further from the truth. I had to watch as people who had known us our whole lives suddenly refused to speak to us, not because of some sin my Father committed, but because they didn't like him standing for truth. Those very people who had been like family not only shunned my parents, but went on an all-out war to destroy them and the ministry work my grandfather started back in the 1940's.

They wrote letters full of hate and lies to destroy the mission's donor base and when that failed to destroy the organization, they lied and stole property that belonged to the organization and pocketed the money, and in the process destroyed thousands of lives.

The reason they gave for their ungodly behavior was because my father was no longer "holy" according to their outward standards. While they maintained their so-called "holy standards," they cheated, lied, spread hate, and did their best to undermine and destroy my father and our mission organization by taking us to court. They claimed the work that was started by my grandfather was theirs. You can read more about his story of being set free from legalism in his books, "Not All Devils Have Horns" and " For Me To Live Is Christ."

The heartbreaking thing was that not only did all that serve to hurt thousands of people we were helping, but it pushed their own children further away from God as well. Many of them, still to this day, have no desire to have anything to do with God because they got sick of the pretense and did not want to serve a God their parents represented.

I recently spoke to one of the men who was responsible for trying to destroy my grandfather's organization. I asked him how his grown kids were, and his answer was sobering. He said, "I don't know. They don't really speak to me."

THE SECRET POWER OF FORGIVENESS

I happen to know how his daughter is because we are friends on Facebook and I pray for her and so many others I grew up with who I know are running from God because of the trauma they experienced in Church.

Many of them don't have a clue who God is and it breaks my heart because they were robbed of a real relationship by a real God who loves them with all His heart. They saw a reflection of what they thought was Him through broken and wounded people unwilling to take the steps to allow Him to heal them.

Part of learning the secret of forgiveness is also being willing to change your view of God from false concepts and let Him teach you the truth of who He really is rather than some abstract concept of a bully in the sky! Recently I heard a story about someone raised in a cult. She was repeatedly raped in the name of God and taught that was who God was or what He willed. My heart broke for her when I heard her story and many more like hers which were based on a false sense of who they thought God was.

My heart also breaks for God because throughout history he has had his reputation tarnished repeatedly by people who valued religion over relationship and claimed to know him but were really working against Him.

If you are someone who has gone through that experience of being hurt by those in the church or believing these false depictions of God, let me say how sorry I am that you have experienced that. Please let me assure you that all those lies about God come straight from the pit of hell. They are meant to rob you of a very real relationship with a God who loves you more than anything.

I finally had to choose to forgive the people who had hurt my earthly parents and also my Heavenly Father and I had to choose to ask God forgiveness for all that I thought He had done wrong to me and allowed "His people to do to me " and ask Him to show me who He truly is.

Thankfully, I chose to do that. I have no clue how I would have gotten through all the pain and heartache I have faced in life had I did not have a real encounter with God. He is now my friend, confidant, wisdom, peace, joy, strength and so much more. All I had to do was seek him.

Chapter 9: Total Wholeness

We are a Spirit having a human experience and when we look at forgiveness, we need to look at it from the whole of our being not just the human aspect of it.

Jesus talked a lot about forgiveness because He wants us to be totally made whole. He paid the price so that might happen. When He was asked how many times we should forgive, He answered, "I tell you not just seven times but seventy-times seven" (Matthew 18:22). NIV. In other words, we are not to stop forgiving but why would Jesus say that? If anyone had understood how hard it was to forgive it certainly would have been Jesus. Yet He asked what seems to be impossible of us. Truthfully it is impossible to truly forgive without the power of the Holy Spirit working in our lives.

Jesus taught us to forgive because there are certain spiritual laws in place that even He can't violate. One of those is the law of sowing and reaping. If we want forgiveness, we must give forgiveness. By choosing to extend forgiveness, it allows us to receive it as well.

Matthew 6:15 and Mark 11:26 both tells us if we choose not to forgive, then God cannot forgive us. The Bible also is very clear that if we don't forgive we cannot expect God to even hear our prayers. Mathew 5:24 says that if we are even bringing a gift to God and remember that someone is upset with us we are to go to them and try and make it right. Wow that seems to be somewhat extreme but there is a reason God ask that of us.

If we want a clear line of communication open to God so we can see the power of the Holy Spirit working in us, we need to be able to stand before Him ourselves with clean hands and a pure heart.

THE SECRET POWER OF FORGIVENESS

As I was writing this book, I was also asking God once again if there was anyone in my life I had not forgiven or who had something against me. God brought someone to my mind who I knew was very angry with me but I was uncertain why. I felt like I should attempt to reach out and see what I could do to fix the situation. Now, let me be clear, choosing to clear the air does not mean you have to allow that individual back into your life and give them room to harm you again. Sometimes in some cases, God can heal the hurt in such away you do want to reconcile and move forward rebuilding relationships but make sure to do so using wisdom and allowing God to lead you as you do. Other times the person may not be repentant, and it would be foolish to expect things to be different and open yourself up to the say kind of hurt or worse. That is when you choose to forgive and allow God to heal your hurt as you move on. Keep in mind some people come into your life for a reason and a season. That is why it is so important to learn the lesson the first time, so you don't have to keep repeating the process.

When God brought the individual to my mind, I obeyed Him and called them and when they answered, I apologized if I had hurt them in any way. The response I got was not only shocking but explained a lot. Almost instantly the individual began to lash out at me and accused me of all sorts of things that were not true. They chose to believe the lies they had heard instead of the truth. If only they had taken the time to hear the truth it would have set them free from years of heartache and bitterness. In that case, I was free before God because I did my best to clear the air, but they didn't want or care to even discuss it.

You see, sometimes there isn't anything you can do to fix a situation but when we choose to forgive and let it go, we experience freedom. Pain may be there, and it might take time to heal but it ultimately sets us on a path to move forward.

Don't be surprised however when you start walking free if people from your past begin to come back around. It's almost as they have some idea that you might be getting set free and want to real you back into their drama. That is when once again you must ask God for wisdom. Especially if you are someone who hates conflict and wants to try and make everything better. There are sometimes in life when you have to get good at loving people from a distance and allow God to heal you and them.

Forgiveness is so important to God that Jesus even taught us to pray it during what many people call the Lord's prayer, Matthew 6:9-13 NIV "forgive us our debts as we forgive our debtors."

So, why is it so important? Besides setting us free, it opens a clear channel for God to hear our prayers and allows heaven to go to work on our behalf.

If we are focused on anger, bitterness, and resentment over what someone did to us, we are not focused on how much God loves us and what He wants to accomplish in our lives. It hinders our prayers when we are in disobedience to what God has said and stops the blessings in our lives.

You can't plead promises and violate principles, it doesn't work that way. God isn't a fairy godmother who just waves a magic wand and regardless of what you do or how you act, just gives you whatever you want. His promises are true, and you can stand on them, but they are for you only if you follow what He says. If you decide to make a cake and throw in only half of the ingredients expecting it to come out right, you will be disappointed. The same is true with God. Many people want all the great things God promises but are not willing to follow the steps to do what God has said in order to see them come to pass.

I know God's promises are true. I have seen them personally come to fruition. Keep an eye out for my next book where I share how God has given me many blessings, including homes, unexpected income, protection, favor, and much more. However, I also know that all that is based on hearing from God and having a real relationship with Jesus and the power of the Holy Spirit operating in my life. In order to have that power you must surrender to fully doing things Gods way.

You will find life is so much more peaceful when you just make the quality decision to do that. Does it mean you won't have any more battles or hardships? No. You may even see them increase. However, the great thing is that you won't be fighting those battles on your own and you will know that God is on your side fighting for you.

THE SECRET POWER OF FORGIVENESS

You will have all of heaven working on your behalf to set things right in your life. When you choose to do things God's way, you can rest assured that there are no hinderances in your life to keep you from hearing God and being daily guided by His Holy Spirit. That will make your life an adventure, one that will take you places you never dreamed of and helps you accomplish things you didn't think were possible. Allowing God to come into your life and being obedient to Him will give you that wholeness you've been longing for. God promises to open doors that no one can shut to bless you when you come in and when you go out, but you have to allow Him to guide you in order to do that.

When I think of communication with God, I think of a glass jar. Pretend it was a jar that was filled with dirt and worms and smashed bugs. Then someone comes and cleans up the outside but the jar is still filthy inside. They then fill it up with something to drink and hand it to you. Would you drink it? Probably Not! You would want it sparkling clean both on the inside and out. Yet so many people live their lives like that. They pretend everything is good with God on the outside but internally they are dealing with so much fear, guilt, and shame that they don't want to even approach God much less try to listen to His voice. Somehow, we have this idea that if we don't come to God, He won't know what we have done. So instead we try to hide from God and that keeps us from being able to even communicate with Him at all.

Communication with God is vital in maintaining that wholesome relationship with Him. In order to stay in His presence, we must always be willing to come clean about any mistakes or transgressions we committed and ask for forgiveness. Even though God already knows everything we think, say, or do, He still wants us to be able to come to Him about it.

I love David in the Bible because he was a mess if there ever was one. He had an affair with Bathsheba, then had her husband killed in battle – all while he was king! He messed up over and over again but each time he went to God about it and repented of his sin. At times David was joyful and others he was angry and upset but through it all he kept the lines of communication open with God. You can read a lot of what David wrote in the Psalms. He chose to be open and transparent with God and evidently God loved that because He called David " a man after his own heart."

That is where grace comes in. Grace is unmerited or undeserved favor with God. It is when God looks past our sin and sees the blood that Jesus shed for us and continues to forgive us. Grace doesn't however give us a license to just freely sin and go against Gods word. A lot of people are preaching the grace message today. I am beyond thankful for God's grace but there comes a point when God expects us to walk in victory and not just barely get through by His grace.

You see, we can't do anything on our own to earn forgiveness or get rid of unwanted sin in our lives. If we could, we wouldn't have needed a Savior and Jesus wouldn't have had to pay the price. We have to have a real relationship with Jesus walking and talking with us and guiding us into all truth. We also must have the power of the Holy Spirit, the gift that Jesus promised when He went back to Heaven.

THE SECRET POWER OF FORGIVENESS

Oftentimes people say to me, "I don't know how you do it." The easy answer is that I know I can't do anything on my own. Most days I get up and don't feel like I can face the responsibilities and the many challenges I have as a mother, pastor, and vice president of a huge mission organization. The only way I manage is because God gives me my strength. He sustains me. He is where the secret power of forgiveness comes from, as well as the power to accomplish anything in life.

Chapter 10: The Power of Forgiveness

Many times people think if they refuse to forgive someone that they are holding that other person accountable or hostage for the pain they inflicted. It gives the hurt individual a false sense of power over the one they think deserves to pay for what they have done. The irony is that the opposite is true. Many times, that is how the enemy does things; he comes to make us believe a lie to keep us bound down because he knows the Truth will set us free.

The reason Jesus commanded us to forgive those who have wronged us is because when we forgive it brings us so many blessings along with physical and spiritual benefits. It also gives us power over the enemy who is doing his best to steal, kill and destroy our lives.

THE SECRET POWER OF FORGIVENESS

God said that when we forgive, then He can hear our prayers. If we know that He hears us and we are praying according to His will, we know that we have what we ask Him for in prayer. However, if we don't forgive others, He can't forgive us and can't hear our prayers.

Forgiveness opens the channels for God to begin to flow through and clean out all the hurt and debris of pain and any other issues that we might have. It also gives a clear line of communication with God when we are walking in right standing with God. That is one big reason why the devil tries so hard to keep us from forgiving because he is afraid what will happen when we walk in unity.

When we stand in unity with other believers, we are unstoppable. The enemy knows that and does everything in his power to keep us bound up with a spirit of offense. He knows that hurt individuals hurt others. So, he does everything he can to keep us focused on the pain from our past. As a result, there a lot of people that are missing out on all their God given potential to change the world around them.

THE SECRET POWER OF FORGIVENESS

It reminds me of a girl I knew. She was married and desperately wanted her husband to plan a fun date or weekend but he would never do it. I suggested she do it and then, after they had a great time, ask him to surprise her and do it the next time. She said no because she did do that one-time many years ago but he didn't respond the way she had hoped so she wasn't going to do it again. From what I could tell, her husband wanted to please her and loved her but had no clue that he offended her years ago and she was still mad about it. Rather than sitting down and talking about this, she continued to be offended, bitter and angry. Just the wrong look from anyone caused her to boil over in anger. She was like a porcupine just waiting for someone to say the wrong thing to her so she could shoot a quill of bitter anger towards them. She was so hurt and mad at the world that she didn't even see it was destroying the very thing she said she wanted, love and a great life. She played the blame game so well and was so busy pointing fingers at everyone around her that, like the porcupine, she was pushing everyone away who tried to help her. The sad fact is, unless she starts taking a long hard look in the mirror, she will end up on a path to self-destruction. Her life will become a self- fulfilling prophecy of everyone out to get her and she will end up alone and miserable.

Another woman I know who is in her late 60's is also filled with so much rage that even her own children do not want to be around her. She has convinced herself that no one likes her and she is pretty much right. She is angry, bitter and not a very nice person to be around. In fact, she spews hate and has set herself up for failure before she even gets somewhere, she has convinced herself that no one will like her when she gets there. She has a whole list of all the wrongs that have been done to her in life and can recite them all by heart if you give her five minutes of your time. Instead of her later years being used to make a difference in the lives of others, she is wallowing in self-pity and driving everyone away while blaming everyone else for the way they are treating her. It is heartbreaking but we all know people like that. We also know people who have every right to be angry and hurt because of what they have been through in life. Yet they chose to forgive and receive the power that comes through the choice of forgiveness and have gone on to accomplish amazing things in life.

THE SECRET POWER OF FORGIVENESS

God created you for a unique purpose and designed you with a Master plan. He longs to empower you to become all that He created you to become in life. Psalms 139 tells us we are fearfully and wonderfully made. Jeremiah 29:11 says that God has great plans for you plans to prosper you and not to harm you. God even wants to give you the desires of your heart and the word desire comes from the Latin word meaning of the Father. So God literally puts into your heart your desires and then wants to fulfill them.

The enemy has been on a mission to destroy that great plan and does everything he can to get you off track or distracted with pain and hurt in your life. The last thing he wants is for you to walk in Victory. He is afraid of all that you will accomplish in your life when you fully realize who God is and who you are in God. You were bought with a price at the very cost of Jesus' life so that you might have a life of abundance and victory in this life and spend eternity with God in the next.

The Bible tells us that Jesus went through and experienced everything we do in life so that he could truly understand what it felt like to go through the pain of this life. It also tells us He is close to the broken-hearted.

The night of a parent-teacher meeting for the school, I sat on the front pew while the hateful words of the parents were hurled at me like rocks. Each one caused me to cringe as I sat there feeling so alone and abandoned in my spirit. All the while I kept hearing a Bible verses about what Jesus went through on his way to the cross. Isaiah 53:7KJV states, "He was oppressed and He was afflicted, Yet He did not open his mouth, Like a lamb that is lead to slaughter and like a sheep that is silent before its shearers, So He did not open his mouth." It goes on to say, " Surely our grief's He Himself bore, and our sorrows He carried." But he was pierced for our transgressions, and he was crushed for our iniquities. The punishment that brought our peace was on him; and by his stripes we are healed.

Later, after some time had passed from that event, I had begun to feel the forgiveness and I asked Jesus, "where were you when I was going through so much pain during that event?" I clearly heard Him reply in my spirit "Sitting beside you. Who do you think was reminding you of all I went through for you?" You see friend, even in the darkest times, of what you faced He was right there with you, holding you, crying with you, and wanting you to know that He will never leave you nor forsake you if you allow Him in your life.

Chapter 11: Choosing Forgiveness

In closing, I want to encourage you to make the choice to fully accept Jesus into your life, if you have not already done so. He wants you to have a life filled with joy, love, and pleasures ever more.

The Christian life is not a life of ease like some people think. It is daily laying down our own natural human way of doing things in surrender to the guidance of the Holy Spirit. It isn't easy but it is so worth it because you have a friend Jesus that sticks closer than a brother to walk along the challenges of life with you.

Religion is about control and Jesus had a lot of choice things to say about the religious leaders of his day. He didn't have much use for them. Many people have rejected Jesus because they think He is about religion, but the truth is that He wants a real relationship with you. A relationship with Him can begin today. God loves you and wants to give you everything your heart is searching for in life. You see, we are all designed with a God-sized hole that only He can fill. Many times, we try to fill that void with everything else. Those things end up breaking our hearts even more and take us down roads that wind up leading us to more despair.

No matter what you have been through or done in your life, God promises that He can come into your heart and make it just as if you never sinned. He can forgive you, cleanse you, and totally make you brand new again. If you have never experienced that, it can be hard to understand but I encourage you to just take the chance and ask Him to come in and cleanse you from all that you have done wrong. It will be the most fulfilling thing you ever experience.

1 John 1:9NLT says, "But if we confess our sins to him, he is faithful and just to forgive us our sins and to cleanse us from all wickedness." Jesus paid the price on the cross so you don't have to; God wants to have a real

relationship with you. He doesn't hold what you have done against you but wants to make you in right standing with Him so He can help you begin afresh and anew.

Ask God to empower you through the Holy Spirit to live a life full of adventure with Him. It is a life that will bring you greater peace and satisfaction than you have ever known. He is able to meet your every need.

So, if you haven't accepted Jesus into your life yet, stop and do it now. All you have to do is talk to Him and ask Him to forgive you to make you new again. Ask Him to show you who He truly is and watch how He begins to transform your life starting today.

If you have accepted Christ in your life but you have been walking around with anger and bitterness still, you need to know you are only hurting yourself. Instead of allowing God to really make a difference in your life, you are giving the enemy room to hold you bound and keep you from all God created you to do.

Don't waste another minute of your life by allowing that dirty rotten devil to win. Decide right now to take back

THE SECRET POWER OF FORGIVENESS

the ground he has stolen from you. We don't fight other people; we fight the devil working through other people to try to destroy us. Don't let him succeed. Tell him to go back to hell where he belongs, and make a quality decision today to choose to follow God's way.

Here is the prayer I pray when someone hurts me or does me wrong. I would suggest you pray it too: I know the devil will try and stop you from praying this prayer, because he doesn't want you set free. Remember it isn't about a feeling but a choice so make that choice now to begin a new today.

Father, I choose as an act of my will to forgive _____ for what they did to hurt me. I submit to you and I resist the devil and I choose to do this Your way. So I chose to forgive_____ and I cut the spiritual cord between us. I give you my half, Father, to fill me up from any hurt or pain I have gone through because of this and I ask you to forgive me for anything I might have knowingly or unknowingly contributed to this event. I also give you their spiritual cord and ask you to work in their life to do what needs to be done to connect them to you. I ask you to help me to continue to choose forgiveness and to heal all the places of pain in my life. I ask you to cut any ungodly soul ties I might have with_____I ask you to totally release me and set me totally free. In Jesus' name I pray, Amen.

When someone deeply hurts us part of our soul gets tied up with theirs and so often we feel fragmented and have constant nagging thoughts about them. When you ask God to cut any ungodly soul ties and make you whole again. It allows Him to take the shattered pieces of your soul and bring you back to a place of Shalom Peace with nothing missing or broken. He will restore you into what He created you to become in Him in the first place.

By praying that prayer, not only will you set yourself free from the person who hurt you but you can ask God to intercede on their behalf as well. Remember, it doesn't let them off the hook, but it allows God to take over and do what He needs to do in their life and in yours

I would encourage you to get some place quiet and make a list of anyone who has hurt you or who you have hurt. Go through each one, praying that prayer. Ask God to heal you and disconnect any soul ties that should not be there. Choose forgiveness for you and for them.

When you do that, you no longer carry the weight of those people. You are free. It may be difficult at times and takes much practice but just continue to make that choice and before you know it, you too will experience the secret power of forgiveness that allows you to live the life you were born to live.

If you have taken these steps, I would love to hear from you. Feel free to contact me on social media under MisfitforJesus or write to me at:

P.O Box 189

Summerfield FL 34491.

Also, I would encourage you to get into a good Bible believing church and begin to really read God's Word. Ask God to show you who He really is, and what He wants to do in you and through you.

THE SECRET POWER OF FORGIVENESS

There are so many things God has taught me through the many challenges of life I have faced. One of those things is He is well able to take all the things we have been through even the times when we deliberately were not following Him and all the messes we get ourselves into and restore everything the enemy has stolen from us. When we surrender our lives, He weaves a map or a tapestry that takes even the biggest hurts and mistakes and turns them into something beautiful to be used mightily by Him. I can now honestly say I am grateful for all the lessons and challenges God has allowed me to walk through. I hope to never repeat those lessons, but they have taught me so much and, in the process, helped me to have an even deeper relationship with my Heavenly Father. Although the things I have walked through have been extremely painful they have assisted me as steppingstones into becoming more of what God created me to become. I have been able to witness firsthand the power of the Holy Spirt working in my own life to transform me. He has helped me to lay down and surrender things to Him that I didn't think I could ever let go. He has taken me from a place of wishing harm on my enemies to not only praying for them but truly wanting Gods best in their lives.

Truthfully, I have had a hard time writing this book because I didn't want to hurt anyone in anyway. But what I have found in God is if we truly commit to doing things His way and walk in obedience to Him. He will use everything we have been through to not only be a blessing to us but to others around us.

God even promise us that the enemy will have to pay back from what he has stolen from us. So, once you commit to doing things His way begin to ask Him to restore back the years, the heartache, and anything else the enemy has stolen from you and watch what God will do.

A little over 12 years ago God asked me to come back to work in the very place where the enemy almost had me end my life. When He did, he told me "I am taking you back to the place of your pain so I can totally heal you." He also told me the reason the devil tried so hard to kill me so many years before was because he was afraid of what I was going to become in God when I discovered my God given identity. I am committed to making the devil pay for all the hell he has put me through, by doing my best to live a life so on fire for God it helps to point others to His love for them. I have also discovered the place of my greatest pain has been used by God to give me my greatest ministry. I have made my choice, now its your turn. Will you make the commitment to living your best life today by learning the secrets that come through the power of forgiveness?

www.ingramcontent.com/pod-product-compliance
Lightning Source LLC
Chambersburg PA
CBHW032128090426
42743CB00007B/509